STYLISH
Découpage

STYLISH
Découpage

15 step-by-step projects to dazzle and delight

MARY MAGUIRE

NEW
HOLLAND

First published in 2004 by New Holland Publishers (UK) Ltd
London • Cape Town • Sydney • Auckland

Garfield House, 86–88 Edgware Road, London W2 2EA, United Kingdom
www.newhollandpublishers.com

80 McKenzie Street, Cape Town 8001, South Africa

14 Aquatic Drive, Frenchs Forest, NSW 2086, Australia

218 Lake Road, Northcote, Auckland, New Zealand

ISBN 1 84330 705 7

1 3 5 7 9 10 8 6 4 2

Senior Editor: Clare Hubbard
Editor: Anna Southgate
Production: Hazel Kirkman
Design: AG&G Books; Glyn Bridgewater and Jane Skinner
Photography: Shona Wood
Editorial Direction: Rosemary Wilkinson

Reproduction by Pica Digital Pte Ltd, Singapore
Printed and bound in Malaysia by Times Offset (M) Sdn. Bhd.

DISCLAIMER
The author and publishers have made every effort to ensure that all instructions given in this book are safe and accurate, but they cannot accept liability for any resulting injury or loss or damage to either property or person, whether direct or consequential and howsoever arising.

CONTENTS

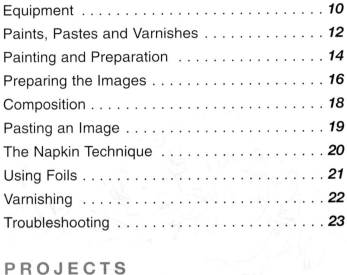

PROJECTS

INTRODUCTION

Découpage is one of the easiest crafts to master and, although it is basically cut and paste, it can be elevated to a fine art through practice, skill and creativity, just like any other craft.

Traditionally, découpage was finished with up to 20 layers of varnish. Each layer would have been sanded before the next was applied, so that a smooth, glossy, lacquer-like finish was achieved. There would be no irregularities on the surface and the pasted-on print could

Right: **This screen has been decorated with shapes cut from origami paper (see page 59).**

be passed off as a painting. The practice originated in Italy, where it was called *lucca contraffatta* (imitation lacquer). The Italians discovered that hand-colouring prints and pasting them on to furniture helped satisfy the demand for the considerably more expensive hand-painted works of great artists. They perfected the technique until it became an art form in its own right. Its popularity spread throughout Europe, and it became a common pastime for

genteel ladies, even nobility: Marie Antoinette is said to have been fond of cutting up her oil paintings and pasting them on to furniture. In fact, it is from French that the word découpage derives.

The craft reached the height of its popularity during the Victorian era, when cheap, mass-produced printed images became available to a wider market. It was so popular that partially cut out images were manufactured specifically for découpage. Many of the designs are still being produced today and some of them appear in this book.

This book offers a series of projects for both novice and proficient découpage artists. Many of them use medium density fibreboard (MDF) blanks, which are made for decorating and are available in craft and hobbyist stores. The same techniques can also be applied to old or second-hand items, providing that all the necessary preparation is carried

Above: **In addition to the MDF blanks available at craft stores, there is a wide range of objects that make ideal surfaces for découpage: small sets of wooden drawers are inexpensive, nicely proportioned and very useful; shoe boxes are easy to get hold of and make very nice gifts, once decorated. Scour junk shops to find unusual items such as lampshades and crockery.**

out beforehand. The advantage of MDF is that it has a smooth finish, no grain and is stable. For the most part, the projects in this book move away from the old, antique look often associated with découpage in favour of a brighter, breezier approach, using a wide range of fresh pastel-coloured paints and floral imagery. Today, most of us are happy to use découpage purely decoratively: we don't want to pretend it is painted on, so the laborious process of applying twenty coats of varnish is not necessary, as long as you make sure you apply enough coats to protect your prints from wear and tear.

Choosing, cutting and creating designs is a fun and relaxing way to spend your time. All sorts of objects can be used as a base, either as an embellishment for your own home or as a gift for someone. Interesting images can be found in magazines and old books, on seed packets, paper napkins, letters, maps and wrapping paper. You can use copyright-free source books, CDs or Victorian scraps. The sources are plentiful. Do respect the copyright laws, however, which are there to protect originators from having their images exploited. Most publishers will be happy to give you permission providing you are not manufacturing items for sale.

MATERIALS

You can use wallpaper, old book illustrations, letters, musical manuscripts, postcards –

the list goes on. If you are reluctant to use originals, scan or colour photocopy them.

1. Wallpaper: Look through wallpaper books to find interesting and funky designs. Ask your local stockist to keep old sample books for you.

2. Wrapping paper: This is probably the most accessible and widely used source material for découpage. It is the right thickness and is available in an abundance of designs.

3. Paper napkins: These have recently become very popular for découpage, and the range of designs is now far greater than ever before. They often have a festive theme, so collect them when you see them as stocks will change to suit the season.

4. Découpage papers: Some craft shops stock papers specially designed for découpage. Designs include musical manuscripts, antique handwriting and images of fishes and birds.

5. Colour photocopies and printouts: If you don't want to use an original image, you can take it along to your local copy shop, where they will colour copy it for you (although this can be expensive). Alternatively if you've got a good scanner and printer you can do it yourself. Experiment with different kinds of paper to find out

which are the best to use. Fabric, feathers and leaves can also all be scanned or copied, but take care not to scratch the surface of the scanner or photocopier.

6. Stickers: These can also be used in découpage, providing they can be varnished over. Test them first.

7. Victorian scraps: There is a wide variety still being produced today (see pages 78–79 for suppliers). These charming, embossed images are already partially cut out, which makes them very easy to use.

8. Foils: Keep your chocolate/sweet wrappers! Smoothed out, they will make sumptuous source material for your designs.

9. Copyright-free source books and CDs: Books containing copyright-free images are available on all sorts of subjects, including Christmas, animals etc. (see pages 78–79 for details).

10. Origami papers: These small, square sheets of paper tend to have miniature patterns on, making them ideal for découpage; see the variation of the Sky Screen on page 59.

STORAGE

It is useful to be able to store any unused cutouts for a later date. Plastic-covered pages from a photo album are ideal for this purpose. They will hold the shapes flat and protect them from dust and damage.

EQUIPMENT

You don't need a lot of equipment for découpage, but if you are intending to do a lot of

it, it is worth investing in good quality brushes, scissors, a cutting mat and a scalpel.

Note: when using any equipment you should always follow the manufacturer's instructions.

1. Muslin: This fine, open-weave, cotton cloth is ideal for wiping newly sanded surfaces.

2. Brushes: It is worth investing in good-quality brushes if you intend to make a hobby of this craft; they won't shed hairs.

3. Roller/brayer: This is useful for flattening down your pasted design and expelling any trapped air bubbles.

4. Sponge: You will need a clean, soft sponge for wiping over a freshly pasted design to remove any surplus paste.

5. Fine brushes: Good-quality fine-headed brushes with broad, flat, blunt ends are especially useful.

6: Cling film: This is handy for covering surfaces in order to protect them from paint, but also for covering pots of paint and paste mixtures to prevent them from drying out as you work.

7. Face-mask: Wear one of these for protection against sanding dust, stray powder particles and fumes when you are spray varnishing.

8. Sponge spreaders: These are useful for spreading paste. Beneath the sponge head, there is a firm plastic core which gives the tool more body.

9. Knife: It is good to have a slim, blunt-ended knife to hand for peeling off unsatisfactory prints.

10. Plastic wallets: These are very useful for storing images.

11. Protractor, pencil and ruler: You will need these for planning out your designs. Choose a hard pencil and make sure the point is sharp.

12. Reusable putty: This is invaluable for positioning images. It enables you to tack elements of your design into place so that you can look at them from a distance.

13. Scalpel: A scalpel is important for cutting out tiny interior areas that are difficult to reach using scissors. Make sure you always use a sharp blade, as blunt ones tend to tear or buckle the paper.

14. Cutting mat: If you do craft work often, you will find a cutting mat useful. Otherwise, improvise with a piece of hard-board, lino or a thick wad of newspaper.

15. Scissors: You will need a pair of scissors with fine, sharp points.

Embroidery scissors are good for cutting out fiddly detail. You will also need a large pair of paper or general-purpose scissors for cutting out larger areas. Keep both of these specially dedicated to découpage.

16. Spatula: Use to smooth out freshly pasted prints, and to expel any trapped air bubbles.

17. Decorators' and masking tape: Decorators' tape is a smooth-surfaced low-tack tape, while masking tape has a slightly crinkled surface. They are both used to mask out areas for painting and for achieving straight lines.

18. Lining paper: Be sure to have a plentiful supply of lining paper, scrap or newspaper before you embark on a project. A new sheet for each pasting is the best way to avoid mishaps.

19. Lazy Susan: A lazy Susan is a round wooden board that revolves on a smaller base. It is very useful for doing craft work, as you can turn your artwork without needing to touch it. A lazy Susan is particularly useful for varnishing – just be sure to cover it with cling film or foil before you start.

20. Mixing bowl: Use old bowls for mixing paint and paste. Plastic ones are good and easy to clean.

21. Cloths: Keep a pile of old cotton cloths around you as you are working so that you can mop up spillages and wipe paintbrushes with minimum effort.

22. Manicure scissors: These are good for cutting out fine detail. They often have curved edges, which also can be ideal. Keep them solely for this purpose!

23: Tweezer scissors: The squeezing action of these very sharp tweezer-like scissors, ensures a fine, smooth cut. They are available with both straight and curved points (see pages 78–79 for suppliers).

24. Cotton wool buds: These are very useful for dabbing away little pockets of glue that collect in awkward places.

25. Cocktail sticks and pins: These can be useful for applying tiny amounts of glue.

26. Dollmaker's needle: This needle is long and straight enough to go through an egg, while the eye is big enough to thread thin ribbon through.

27. Sandpaper: Available at hardware and DIY stores, it comes in a range of gauges from coarse to very fine. For sanding between layers of paint use a very fine paper; for stripping off old paint use a coarse paper. If in doubt, ask for advice at your local hardware store.

PAINTS, PASTES AND VARNISHES

Many different kinds of paint can be used for découpage. I've chosen to use emulsions as they come in a wide range of colours and can be bought inexpensively in small tester pots.

Note: when using any product you should always follow the manufacturer's instructions.

1. Spray varnish: Although this is more expensive than conventional varnish, it is quicker to apply and the drying time is very fast. It is available in matt, gloss and satin finishes. The projects in this book were made using either Plaka matt varnish or a triple gloss varnish.

2. Decorators' varnish: This product has been devised especially for fine decorative finishes. It is a thin, milky, water-based liquid, available in a dead flat finish as well as satin and gloss.

3. Tissue paste: This is a light paste, manufactured solely for use with napkins.

4. High-gloss varnish: Most of the projects were created using water-based paints and varnishes. For a really glossy finish a varnish devised for polymer clay is recommended.

5. Wallpaper paste: Although useful for projects made with wallpaper, this is also good for making up your own découpage paste mix (see page 19 for details).

6. PVA glue: This general-purpose glue can be used neat on heavier papers, or mixed with wallpaper paste for use on lighter papers.

7. Sticks: These are extremely useful for mixing paints and paste. Make sure they are smooth and will not shed bits of bark into your paint.

8. Bronze powders: These are extremely fine metallic powders, which can be mixed with a special medium, PVA glue or varnish to give a metallic finish or lustre to a piece. They are available in a sumptuous range of colours including purple, green and blue.

9. Three-dimensional paints: These squeezable bottles of paint come complete with nozzle lids, which enable you to pipe out decoration. The paint stays raised once dry – like icing – and gives an embossed effect to your work. They are available in a range of colours and finishes, including metallic, pearl and sparkle. You can buy them from craft stores.

10. Acrylic paint: These small pots of paint can be used to paint eggs. They come in a range of pretty, pale, pastel colours.

11. Primers: Use white primer for projects with light finishes and grey for darker ones. I have used water-based primers, which are suitable to go under emulsion paints, and are easier to wash out of brushes.

12. Felt-tipped pens: If you want to add a bit more colour to your prints, to colour in black and white prints, or to make the white edges of cutouts disappear, you can use felt-tipped pens. You can get these in subtle colours from good art supply shops. Before using them, test them out with paste and varnish to make sure the colours don't bleed.

13. Emulsion paints: Available in a much wider selection of colours than oil-based paints, these have the added advantage that you can buy them in small tester pots. These water-based paints are relatively quick-drying. They are easy to use but must be protected using a varnish.

PAINTING AND PREPARATION

It is worth spending time on preparation. The finished product will look better and will

last longer, but it does require practice and patience.

Whether you are using a new MDF blank or an old wooden or painted object, all of the surfaces must be sanded smooth: varnish magnifies any imperfections in the paintwork. Even with MDF blanks, there are often gaps where the surfaces haven't quite joined smoothly. These can be filled using decorators' filler. If you are decorating older or antique items, you might find wormholes or scratches. You may wish to keep these to add character, but if not, they can be filled using wood filler.

SANDING

Sandpapers come in various grades and, depending on your surface, you will need to select accordingly. For most of the MDF items in this book, I have used a silicone carbide 400-grit paper. If you are working on wood or previously painted surfaces, you will probably need coarser paper. Ask your local DIY merchant for advice. It helps to wrap your sandpaper around a

small block of wood, as this will give you a better grip. If your fittings (hinges or catches) are on the surface and visible, you may want to remove them until the painting is complete. An alternative option is to cover them with masking tape to protect them. Always wear a face-mask when sanding.

PRIMING

Priming seals the surface of an object prior to painting. For all of the projects in this book, I have used a water-based primer – white for light finishes and grey for dark. Before you start priming, remove the surface dust with a muslin cloth, then paint the surface with a smooth, even layer of primer. When working on wood, always brush in the direction of the grain.

PAINTING

When painting an object with recesses, it is always best to start from the inside and paint outwards. Before you start, stir the paint

gently to make sure it is mixed thoroughly. Do not shake the tin, as this will cause air bubbles. For the majority of projects in this book I have used emulsion paint, which is then sealed with varnish. You will need a broad, flat brush to spread the paint evenly over the surface.

SANDING PAINTWORK
Once the paint has dried thoroughly, it will need a light sanding. This will smooth out any irregularities and get rid of the more obvious brush marks. Rub over the surface with a dry, soft muslin cloth to mop up any paint dust before applying a second coat of paint. Always wear a face-mask when sanding.

BRONZE POWDERS

MASKING

To mask out a specific area – say for a border – use low-tack decorators' tape. If you need to mask a curve, cut slots along one edge of the tape at 1 cm (½ in) intervals, and ease the tape around the curve.

EMBOSSING

These are fine metallic powders, and are available in a surprising range of colours, in addition to the obvious gold, silver or bronze. They can be mixed with a special medium, or alternatively with PVA glue or varnish. The trick is to get an even suspension of powder in the liquid so that the particles are well distributed once painted (see photograph above). These powder particles are very fine and you should wear a face-mask when using them, taking care to disturb the powder as little as possible.

Paint the metallic mix on smoothly. Try not to overlap areas, as you will get a denser distribution of powder (see photograph below).

Use a three-dimensional paint to embellish a design. The paint tube has a long nozzle that acts like an icing bag. Regularly check the nozzle isn't blocked with dried paint. If it is, you can usually dislodge the blockage using a pin. Leave plenty of drying time after applying a three-dimensional paint.

PREPARING THE IMAGES

Before you start, it is essential that you have a good pair of sharp scissors. Furthermore,

any paper that isn't colourfast will need to be sprayed first with a fixative or varnish.

This will ensure that the colours don't bleed during the gluing or varnishing stages. Hold the can 20 cm (8 in) away from the paper and spray evenly over the surface. A clever trick is to spray very lightweight papers, which makes them more robust for cutting and pasting.

ISOLATING IMAGERY

When cutting an image from a busy pattern, it helps to isolate it first by drawing around it.

CUTTING OUT "INTERIOR" AREAS

Small, fiddly areas are best cut out before the whole isolated image is cut from a sheet of paper. This will give you greater stability and reduces the risk of tearing. Use a self-healing mat and a scalpel. Check that the blade is sharp – a blunt blade will tear the paper. (See photograph above right.)

GENERAL CUTTING

Cut out an isolated image using a medium-to-large pair of scissors. Take care not to cut across any image you might want to use later (see photograph right).

CUTTING EDGES

You will need to use a small pair of scissors for cutting the final outline edges of an isolated image. Manicure scissors are good for this. Practise on magazine images. Cut around your shape, directing the scissors from beneath the paper so that only the points are visible. This will make it easier for you to see where you are cutting. Hold the scissors with a relaxed hand, tilted upwards (gives the edge of the paper a slight bevel). Guide the paper into the blades, reserving the tips for intricate edges. Every so often, cut off surplus paper and discard. (See photograph right.)

CUTTING CURVES TO FIT OBJECTS

There are two ways of doing this. The first is by placing your object on top of the print in the desired position, and tracing along the curve with a pencil. This can then be cut. The second method, shown here, is to tack the image into position, use your finger to rub along the edge of your object – its shape will be embossed on to the paper – and then you can cut it out.

INTERLOCKING IMAGES

If your final composition involves several different shapes that abut each other, you may want to make sure that the images line up neatly without gaps, instead of merely overlapping. This can be done quite simply, by cutting an excess amount at the end of each shape at the

point at which it should meet another. Line two such shapes up on the cutting surface, each with a slight overlap. Stabilize them with tiny bits of reusable putty, and cut through both overlapping prints along the line you want to join.

Make sure your blade is sharp and that you do cut through both prints completely. You will need to press down firmly to secure the prints and prevent any movement.

THICKENING FINE LINES

This is a useful tip for helping to cut out fine lines. Before cutting, choose a crayon or felt-tip pen (make sure it is colourfast) the same colour as the image to be cut out and colour around fine lines to thicken them up. (See photo below.)

LOSING WHITE EDGES

If your cutout images are dark and they are going to be stuck onto dark backgrounds, the white edges of the paper will show up. To get rid of these white edges, use a colour felt-tip pen or crayon that matches either the print or the background. Check first for colourfast compatibility with your varnish.

COMPOSITION

Beauty is in the eye of the beholder, and only you can decide what composition will please you. Spend time shuffling your prints around until you achieve an appealing arrangement.

Don't rush this process – it's better to spend time getting it right at this stage rather than having to peel off an unsatisfactory design later on.

BACKGROUND

For a design with many different elements, first decide what is going to be used as the background. This will tend to be the largest of your cutouts. Tack down this image first, using reusable putty.

CREATING A RHYTHM

Build up the design with smaller elements. Here, smaller blossoms have been added to give the design a circular or wreath-like quality.

FOREGROUND ELEMENTS

Start to place the elements in the foreground, tacking them in place with reusable putty as you go. Be careful not to overwhelm the background. Generally, more detailed images will be in the foreground. (See photo right.)

MARKING POSITIONS

Using a sharp pencil, lift the edges of the tacked prints slightly away from the surface so that you can mark out their positions with a dotted line – just to the inside of where the edge will lie – so once pasted, the marks will not show.

PASTING AN IMAGE

Once you are certain of a composition, and have it clearly marked out on your object,

you can begin to paste the prints into position.

Always use a new sheet of newspaper for each pasting. The thickness of the glue you use will depend on what type of paper you are gluing – a heavier, thicker, paper will require a thicker paste, while tissue paper needs a thinner mix. Many of the découpage glues on the market have a PVA base.

MIX A PASTE

Following the manufacturer's instructions, mix up some wallpaper paste in a jar or pot with a fitted lid (you will probably only need to use a fraction of the packet depending on how much découpage you are doing). Once this is mixed, roughly add an equal quantity of PVA glue and mix thoroughly until the two are completely blended. The wallpaper paste will give the resulting mix a more slimy texture; this allows more leeway when positioning the prints, as neat PVA glue tends to adhere too quickly.

APPLYING THE PASTE

Lay the print, image-side down, on a sheet of scrap paper and spread the glue evenly, making sure that it reaches all edges. Don't worry if you go over the edges, but don't move your print, as the paste may get onto the front of the image and pull off the surface colour. Set the print into position. Smooth it out from the centre with your fingers. Use a spatula to help spread the image and to force out any excess glue. Be careful not to press too heavily, or you may scrape off the surface of your print. (See photo above.)

REMOVING EXCESS GLUE

Remove excess glue by wiping over your object with a barely damp sponge. Repeat until all the surface glue has been removed. (See photo above right.)

TRAPPED GLUE

Any paste trapped in "cutaway islands" can be removed with the tip of a cotton wool bud.

THE NAPKIN TECHNIQUE

This popular technique is finding ever more applications. The source material is taken from paper napkins, which are now available in a vast range of pretty and varied designs.

Only the surface layer of the tissue is used – it is very fine, which makes it ideal for découpage.

SEPARATING THE TISSUE

Napkins are usually constructed from three layers of tissue paper. Only the top layer has a printed image. To peel apart the layers, start at any corner and separate the layers out. Pull them apart gently, taking care not to tear them.

TEARING AND CUTTING

Cut out an image using a small pair of scissors. If you prefer a frayed-edge look, tear out the image instead. First fold and crease along the required border or edge with your fingertip. Then, supporting the tissue on both sides of the crease, tear little by little.

PASTING

Apply a thin layer of paste directly on to the object, rather than on to the tissue. Spread the paste over an area slightly larger than that of your design and gently lay the tissue image on top, smoothing carefully with your fingertips.

BRUSHING OUT

Use your brush to gently spread out the design. Take care, as wet tissue can easily tear.

WORKING ON A DOMED SURFACE

When working on a curved surface, such as an egg, you will need to accommodate all of the baggy excess paper. Because the tissue is so fine, it will easily form pleats with careful brushing.

PASTING LARGER DESIGNS

If your design is fairly large, first wipe it gently to mop up any excess paste. Then lay a barely damp cloth over the surface and go over the image with a roller.

USING FOILS

Foil sweet wrappers are a fantastic resource and can be used to stunning effect in

découpage. Care must be taken when varnishing them, as solvents can dissolve the

coloured surface. Use a water-based varnish or experiment with others. Some craft and

hobbyist shops will stock a range of coloured foils.

SMOOTHING FOIL

TEARING FOIL

If you want your foil design to have rough edges, first draw the shape onto the back of the foil, leaving indented lines, which you can then tear along. If you want a neater design, cut along the indented line instead. (See photo below left.)

APPLYING FOIL

Foil should be stuck down using PVA glue. Take care when applying foil as it tears very easily and also the surface colour can be scratched. Use tweezers to position very small pieces of foil.

Lay your foil, colour-side up, on a smooth surface and gently stroke across the foil until it is smooth. Don't apply excess pressure or you may stretch or tear the foil. For larger pieces of foil, you can use an iron to remove the creases.

VARNISHING

For most of the projects in this book, four coats of varnish will be sufficient. However, some items will need more protection from wear and tear, so allow at least six coats.

The Polka-dot Tray (see page 48) and the Chintz Chairs (see page 64) are examples of items that will need at least six coats. If you want to achieve a finely "lacquered" finish, you will need to sand between the layers of varnish. To achieve a smooth surface, rub harder over any areas where there are lumps or dust, but take great care not to rub through to your design. Wipe off any dust particles with a soft, barely damp, cloth. Once dry, repeat the process, sanding between every second coat, until you have the surface you are happy with.

Spray varnishes speed up the process. They are more expensive, but are better for irregular shapes such as eggs. Whether you use a water-based or spirit-based, matt, satin or gloss varnish, is mostly a matter of taste. Experiment on leftover print scraps. Polyurethane tends to darken prints, and yellows slightly with age, which can be good if you want an antique effect.

APPLYING VARNISH

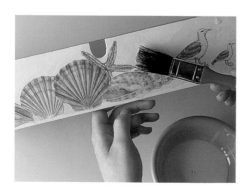

It is important to remember that many thin coats of varnish are better than a few thick ones.

Apply your varnish with a good-quality, flat, blunt-ended brush that will not shed hairs. Choose the size in relation to the object you are working on. Dip the tip of the brush into the varnish; don't overload it, as it will drip. Hold the brush at a 45-degree angle. Lightly drag the brush over the surface of your object. Work away from the centre of the piece, in the same direction as the wood grain, leaving a smooth even coat. Then leave to dry thoroughly. Find a box large enough to cover your object to protect it from dust while it is drying.

VARNISHING AN EGG

If you don't want to use a spray varnish (see right), place reusable putty over the holes in the egg and insert a pushpin in the hole at each end. Use these to support and revolve the egg on a reel of tape as shown. Check that the egg clears the surface.

USING A LAZY SUSAN

If you have a lazy Susan, it can come in handy when varnishing. You can turn an object without getting fingerprints on it. Cover it with a piece of foil or cling film to protect its surface while you work.

SPRAY VARNISHING

When using a spray varnish, it is useful to put your object on the lazy Susan, and place it inside a card-board box. (Suspend eggs from the top of the box.) Wear a face-mask to protect yourself from fumes. Slowly revolve the stand as you spray. The box will help stop the varnish particles dispersing, and will prevent dust from settling on your object.

TROUBLESHOOTING

Take care with each stage of a project, and try not to rush any of the processes

involved. This way, you will avoid making mistakes.

It is advisable to test the compatibility of your materials from the start. (Will the paper react to the glue? Does it stretch terribly? Does the varnish change its colour or opacity?) Most mistakes are easily rectified, and if they can't be, then you can always add other smaller images over the top to camouflage them.

AIR BUBBLES

If an air bubble forms while you are gluing, gently peel back the print until you reach the bubble. Apply a little more glue and, using a spatula, ease the print back into place. If you discover the air bubble after the print is dry, use a sharp scalpel and cut along the nearest contour in your design to reach it. Lift the print carefully with the edge of your scalpel and apply some glue to the underside with a cocktail stick or pin. Then ease the print down, stroking out any air, and wiping away excess glue with a damp sponge. Allow it time to dry completely.

TEARS

Generally, when a wet print tears, it doesn't happen in a straight line, but in a crooked line, usually with one side of the tear showing the white underside of the paper. This actually makes it easier to repair. Peel away the area involved and then re-paste the torn side with the visible underside first. Apply minimal glue along this white edge, and place the other half of the tear on top, matching up the design. Lightly smooth it into place with a damp cloth, taking care not to move it out of alignment.

PEELING IMAGES

This tends to happen along the edges of an image, where insufficient paste has been used. Take a scalpel and lift the peeling edge slightly, then force neat PVA underneath with a pin, brush or cocktail stick. Press down firmly, and maintain pressure for some time. Wipe off any excess glue. It may be necessary to place a weight (such as a telephone directory) over the area to ensure the

edge stays down. Always place a piece of cloth over the image first, however, to protect your work.

REMOVING A PRINT

If, before varnishing, you decide you don't like your design, do not despair. You can completely remove it. Use a warm, damp sponge or cotton bud to soften the glue at the edges of an image first. Then, using a fine, blunt edge, such as a spatula or palette knife, slide under the image and gently lift it bit by bit. Continue working in this way until you have completely removed the design. Any paper residue can be sanded off once the object is dry again.

FEATHERWEIGHT LAMPSHADE

Feathers add to the beauty of these stylishly simple lamps. Feathers can be scanned or

colour photocopied, as can flowers, leaves and shells (providing they are not too bulky).

However, take care not to scratch your scanner or the photocopier.

YOU WILL NEED

- Selection of attractive bird feathers
- Sheet of card or paper 297 x 210 mm (11¾ x 8¼ in)
- Reusable putty
- Scissors
- Cutting surface
- Scalpel
- Lamp with plain fabric lampshade
- Paste (see page 19)
- Paintbrush

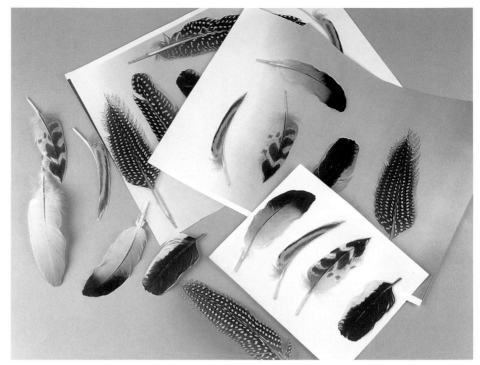

1 Tack the feathers down on to a piece of card or paper using reusable putty. Make sure it is not visible. Scan the page or take it to your local copy shop in a folder for a colour copy.

2 Cut out the general shape of each feather with scissors, then place on a cutting surface to cut out the fine detail using a scalpel.

ARTIST'S TIP

If you want to use the same feather you can make multiple copies on your computer.

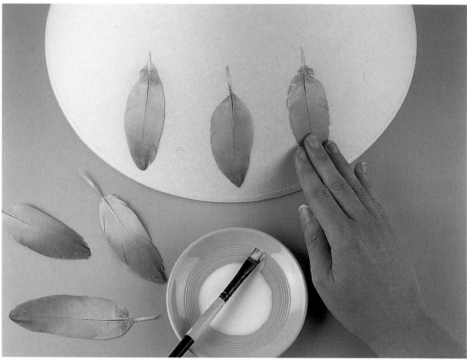

3 Using reusable putty, tack your feathers around the lampshade at regular intervals. Walk away from the piece to view it from a distance. Make any necessary adjustments to achieve a harmonious design.

4 Paste each feather into position in turn, taking care not to get any glue on the exposed areas of the shade. You may need to hold them down for a while until they adhere properly, as gluing on to a curved surface needs a little more care.

DESIGN VARIATION

Fairies are lovely to have on a lamp in a child's room. The light will illuminate them.

SWEET CHERRY COATHANGERS

Simple wooden hangers are impressively transformed with a lick of paint and some

cheerful images cut from wrapping paper. They are a nice gift for a child or teenager.

This is a good project for newcomers to découpage.

YOU WILL NEED

- Wooden coathanger
- Fine sandpaper
- Face-mask
- Muslin cloth
- Water-based primer
- Paintbrushes
- Yellow emulsion paint
- Cherry wrapping paper
- Tweezer scissors
- Paste (see page 19)
- Sponge
- Water-based varnish

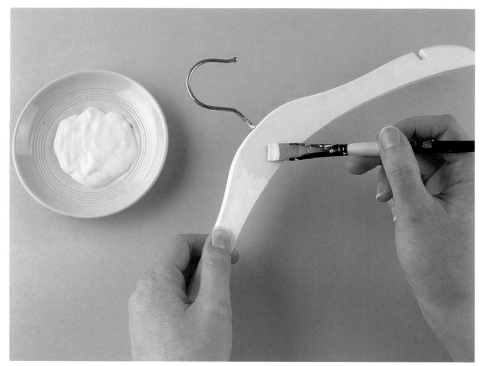

1 Sand off any existing varnish or paintwork from the coat hanger, remove the dust with a muslin cloth and prime the wood. Once dry, apply the emulsion.

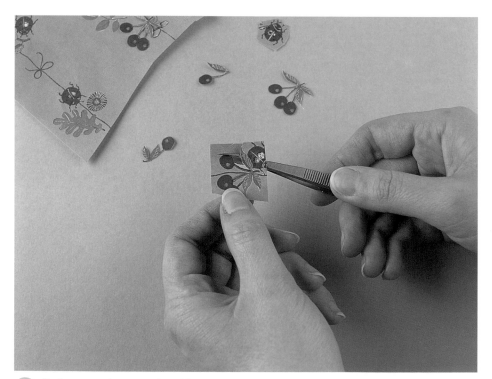

2 Before cutting out the découpage images, check whether any areas need thicker lines drawn on (see page 17) then cut out with small tweezer scissors.

3 Use a brush to apply paste to the back of the image, then position it on your fingertip and place it on the hanger. Wipe over the image with a slightly damp sponge, removing any excess paste, and leave to dry. Paste on further images until you are happy with the result.

4 Once dry, paint a layer of varnish over the hanger. Apply a second coat when the first is dry, and sand again when dry. Repeat the process with another two coats of varnish.

ARTIST'S TIP

It may help to put masking tape around the wire handle to avoid getting paint on it.

DESIGN VARIATION

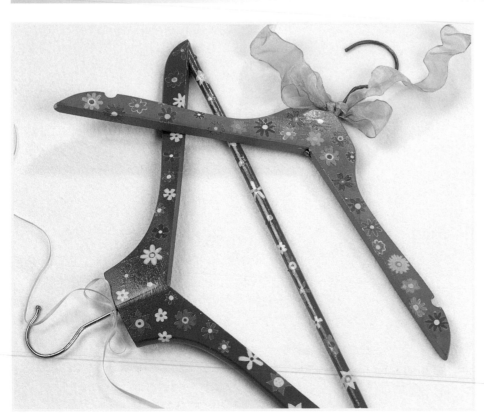

For a teenager choose bright, zingy colours and cut flowers from a sheet of wrapping paper. (See also the variations on page 27.)

PATCHWORK FRAME

This project uses a napkin with a pretty pink patchwork design. If you cannot find

something similar, you can create your own "patches" by cutting up squares of different

patterned paper and fitting them together. Alternatively, you could use fabric, but be sure

to use fine, tightly woven cotton.

YOU WILL NEED

- Paper napkin
- Wooden mirror frame
- Pencil and ruler
- Cutting surface and scalpel
- Water-based primer
- Paintbrushes
- Masking tape (optional)
- Hot pink and pastel pink emulsion paints
- Fine sandpaper
- Face-mask
- Muslin cloth
- Paste (see page 19)
- Sponge spreader
- Cloth
- Roller
- Water-based varnish

1 Measure the napkin against your wooden frame and work out what size border you will need to fit it. Then cut out the centre of the napkin on your cutting surface, using a scalpel and ruler. Prime the wooden frame.

2 Once dry, use a pencil and ruler to mark where you want your inner and outer painted borders to be. For crisp lines, use masking tape to protect the areas you do not want painted. Colour the inner border first, using the hot pink emulsion paint, making sure you don't forget the inner edge.

3 Paint the outer border, including the outside edge of the frame. When dry, give the paint a light sand, wipe away any dust with a muslin cloth and apply a second coat to each border.

4 Remove the backing layers of tissue from the napkin. Apply paste to the appropriate area of the painted frame using a sponge spreader.

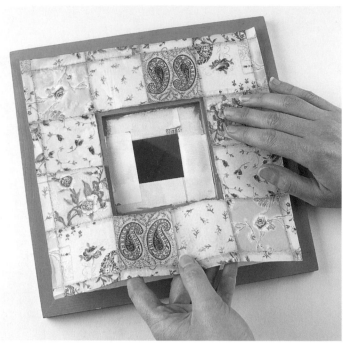

5 Carefully lay the print in position. Smooth out the tissue very gently with your fingers, taking care not to tear the paper. Lay a barely damp cloth over the print and roll across it with the roller. Cut a motif from the leftover napkin and put in each corner of the frame.

6 Once the tissue is dry, paint pastel pink stripes around both borders and leave to dry. Apply six coats of varnish, sanding between layers two and four.

LETTER RACK

Remind yourself of holidays on distant shores with this letter rack. Save postcards of

your favourite places or collect vintage cards. You don't have to use the original; you can

colour copy or scan and print them, reducing them to 50 per cent size to fit your project.

YOU WILL NEED

- MDF letter rack blank
- Fine sandpaper
- Face-mask
- Muslin cloth
- Water-based primer
- Paintbrushes
- Blue emulsion paint
- Selection of holiday postcards
- Scissors
- Reusable putty
- Pencil and ruler
- Paste (see page 19)
- Sponge
- Water-based varnish

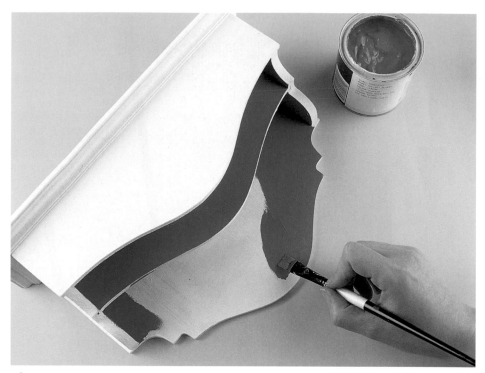

1 Lightly sand the blank letter rack and wipe off any dust with a muslin cloth. Prime the piece and leave to dry, then paint with two layers of blue emulsion. Sand between dry coats to get a really smooth finish.

2 Scan your postcards and reduce to 50 per cent size. Print out or colour copy the images and cut them out using a pair of scissors.

3 Using reusable putty, tack your prints to the letter rack at jaunty angles until you have achieved a pleasing arrangement. Mark out the positions using a sharp, hard pencil and ruler.

4 Paste each postcard into place, carefully using a damp sponge to smooth out the images and remove excess glue. Leave to dry. Once the glue is dry, apply four layers of varnish, sanding after each second coat.

ARTIST'S TIP

Fifties postcards can be bought cheaply from flea markets and vintage stores.

DESIGN VARIATION

For a totally different effect, paint the letter rack in a pale colour and use images of angels.

SCRUMPTIOUS PLATTER

Bronze powders give a metallic lustre to this MDF blank plate. Chocolates, cut from a

sheet of wrapping paper, have been used for decoration, but you could also use images

from advertisements in magazines. The surface on the plate has been finished with a

spray gloss varnish. Take care when you clean this piece – use a damp cloth, but don't

put it in the washing-up bowl!

YOU WILL NEED

- MDF blank plate
- Fine sandpaper
- Face-mask
- Muslin cloth
- Water-based primer
- Paintbrushes
- Russet emulsion paint
- PVA glue
- Bronze powders (fire copper and purple)
- Chocolate wrapping paper
- Scissors
- Coloured pencil or felt-tip pen
- Pencil
- Paste (see page 19)
- Sponge
- Spray gloss varnish

1 Lightly sand the MDF blank until smooth all over and wipe off any dust with a muslin cloth. Prime the plate and leave to dry.

2 Apply two coats of emulsion, sanding between the dry layers.

3 Mix a thin solution of PVA glue and fire copper bronze powder and lightly brush it around the border of the plate. Try to get an even distribution of the powder. Leave the plate to dry.

4 Make a second, denser, mixture of PVA glue with bronze powder – this time purple. Use this to paint a thin edge around the rim of the plate and leave to dry.

5 Cut out the chocolates for your decoration. It is best to cut out more than you need, so that you can play around with the design until you achieve a pleasing result. Colour the edges of your cutouts with a similar coloured pencil or felt-tip pen (see page 17). Mark the final positions of the images with a sharp, hard pencil.

ARTIST'S TIP

If you can't find wrapping paper with chocolates on, look at confectionery wrappers and boxes of chocolates.

6 Apply paste to the back of the prints one at a time, and place them in their marked positions. Start with the most centrally positioned images, then radiate outwards. Wipe off excess paste with a slightly damp sponge. Once completely dry, spray-varnish the plate, wearing a facemask. Apply four coats, lightly sanding every second layer. Once the top is complete, don't forget to do the underside!

SEASHORE DRAWERS

It's not hard to transform a plain set of wooden drawers into a stylish piece of furniture.

This project uses a combination of images taken from wrapping paper, napkins and

images from an old bird book. The effect is to re-create a seaside scene.

YOU WILL NEED

- Small set of wooden drawers
- Fine sandpaper
- Face-mask
- Muslin cloth
- Water-based primer
- Paintbrushes
- White and cream emulsion paints
- Shell wrapping paper
- Scissors
- Reusable putty
- Pencil
- Paste (see page 19)
- Spatula
- Sponge
- Seashore napkins
- Birds' egg colour copies
- Dead flat decorators' varnish

1 Remove the drawers and give all surfaces a light sand before priming, wiping away any sanding dust with a muslin cloth first. Once the primer is dry, paint the drawers with white emulsion, and the cabinet with cream. Leave to dry. Apply a second layer and lightly sand until smooth.

2 Cut out the shells from the wrapping paper and tack to the base drawer using reusable putty. Mark their positions with a sharp pencil. Then, one by one, paste them into position, smoothing out the paper with a spatula, and removing excess paste with a slightly damp sponge. Add a seagull, cut from a seashore napkin.

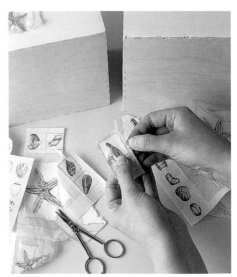

3 Tear out more images from the seashore napkins, following the instructions on page 20, and remove the backing tissue. Decide on an arrangement for the remaining drawers then paste the appropriate areas and apply the tissue on top of the paste, one by one, smoothing out carefully with a paintbrush.

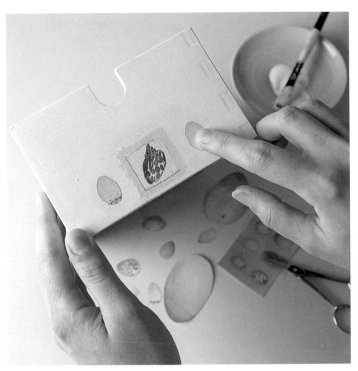

4 Cut out the birds' egg colour copies and paste into position to complement your arrangement.

5 Leave to dry, then coat the cabinet and drawers with dead flat decorators' varnish. This will give it a subtle finish. Apply four coats, lightly sanding between every second layer.

DESIGN VARIATION

This romantic set of drawers is painted in hot pink and purple. Flower wrapping paper surrounds it and Victorian scrap, bunches of flowers decorate the drawers.

MAGAZINE RACK

The image on the front of this funky magazine rack has been cut out from leftover

wallpaper. You can find similar images on the sides of carrier bags. Ask your wallpaper

stockist to keep old sample books for you; they are a great resource for découpage.

YOU WILL NEED

- MDF blank or old magazine rack
- Fine sandpaper
- Face-mask
- Decorators' filler
- Muslin cloth
- Water-based primer
- Paintbrushes
- Coral, hot pink and yellow emulsion paints
- Two large flower prints
- Scissors
- Reusable putty
- Pencil
- Paste (see page 19)
- Spatula
- Sponge
- Cotton wool bud
- Water-based varnish

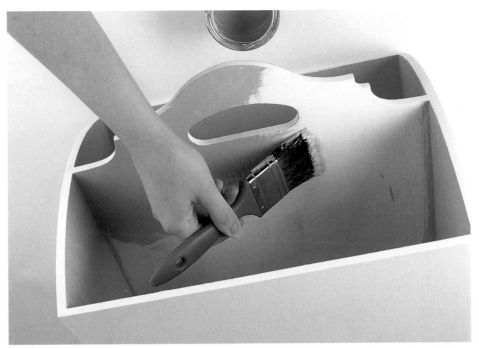

1 Check that your MDF blank is smooth and that the joints are tight. If it is rough in places, sand it before priming. If there are gaps in the joints, fill them with decorators' filler, sand and wipe with muslin, then prime. Once the top is dry, don't forget to prime the base. Paint the inside of the rack first – starting with the inside base – using the coral emulsion. It helps to have a long-handled brush for this job (such as a radiator brush). Leave the paint to dry, then lightly sand before applying a second coat.

2 Once the inside paintwork is dry, you can start on the outside using the hot pink emulsion. Stand the rack on a piece of wood or similar to enable you to paint all around the bottom edge. Apply two coats.

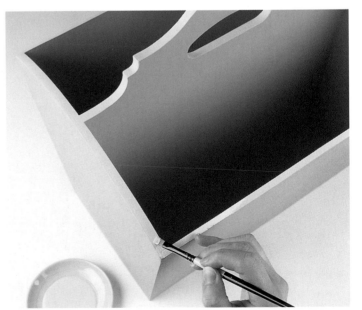

3 When the hot pink emulsion has dried completely, paint the edges of the magazine rack yellow. Apply two coats. Once all the paintwork is dry, lightly sand the rack for a smooth finish.

4 Cut out your design carefully and tack it in position with reusable putty so that you can view it from a distance. When you are sure of its position, carefully mark around it with a pencil.

5 Spread paste onto the back of the print and position it on the rack. Smooth out any wrinkles with a spatula, radiating out from the centre. Wipe over with a slightly damp sponge to remove excess paste. Use a cotton wool bud to remove any paste trapped between the "valleys" of the petals. Repeat this process on the opposite side of the rack.

6 Apply varnish to the finished rack, first to the inside and then to the outside. Once dry, give a light sand and repeat for the second coat. Apply six coats of varnish, lightly sanding between every second coat.

ARTIST'S TIP

Cover the rack with a big box when you are waiting for each layer of varnish to dry to stop dust settling on it.

EASTER EGGS

It is an old Easter tradition to blow eggs and decorate them to hang on a branch. These lovely eggs have been pasted with images cut from Easter napkins (their thin tissue easily moulds around an egg's curved surface) and have been painted with pastel acrylic paints and hung from bright silk ribbons.

YOU WILL NEED

- Blown white eggs (see Artist's Tip)
- Easter paper napkins
- Scissors
- Paste (see page 19)
- Paintbrushes
- Pastel acrylic paints
- Eggcup
- String
- Large box
- Spray varnish (matt or gloss)
- Face-mask
- Long dollmaker's or upholstery needle
- Thin silk ribbon

ARTIST'S TIP

Using a needle, scratch a small cross at each end of the egg. Gradually etch the shell until you have created a small hole in the centre of the cross. Jab around inside the egg with a long needle to break up the yolk, then blow from the broadest end of the egg. Once the egg is empty, wash it in soapy water (making sure the inside of the egg is thoroughly washed). Rub the surface of the egg with vinegar.

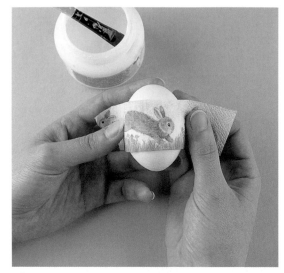

1 Choose your images from the napkins. Cut or tear them out and peel off the backing tissue (see page 20). Decide on the position of your images, then spread paste over the appropriate area on the egg, holding it carefully with your thumb and index finger at either end of the egg. Place the image on the glue and smooth out with a paintbrush (see page 20).

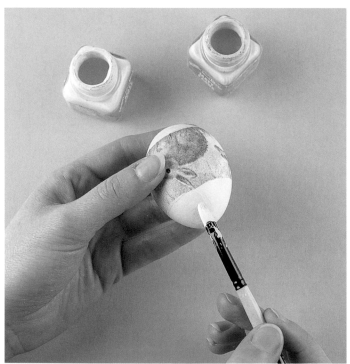

2 Once the glue is dry, you can paint the egg. Start by painting one end with a base colour. Place the egg in an eggcup, the painted end uppermost, and leave it to dry. Repeat on the other end of the egg.

3 Using a fine brush, paint stripes of colour around the one end. Once dry, decorate these with patterns. Paint a flower around the end hole. Repeat at the opposite end.

4 When the body of the egg has been decorated, suspend it on a string in a large box and spray varnish in a well-ventilated room, wearing a facemask, or paint on varnish as described on page 22. When the varnish is dry, using the dollmaker's needle, thread up your silk ribbon and work it through from the bottom of the egg to the top. Make a loop at the top, and thread the needle back through the egg, tying the two ends of the ribbon in a knot at the bottom. Make sure that the knot is big enough not to slip into the egg.

DESIGN VARIATION

Blue and white is such a popular colour to collect crockery in, so why not decorate some eggs to match? These motifs have all been cut from napkins.

POLKA DOT TRAY

Roses and polka dots are a very fashionable combination, and for this project I have found an easy alternative to painting dots. White self-adhesive "dot" stickers have been stuck in position around the tray's sides. The roses are Victorian scraps (see pages 78–79 for details). Ensure that you don't stint on the layers of varnish for this project, as trays have to stand up to a lot of wear and tear.

YOU WILL NEED

- MDF blank tray
- Fine sandpaper
- Face-mask
- Muslin cloth
- Water-based primer
- Paintbrushes
- Decorators' tape
- Blue, pink and white emulsion paints
- White self-adhesive dot labels
- Pencil
- Small scissors
- Victorian rose scraps
- Paste (see page 19)
- Sponge
- Spatula
- Matt water-based varnish

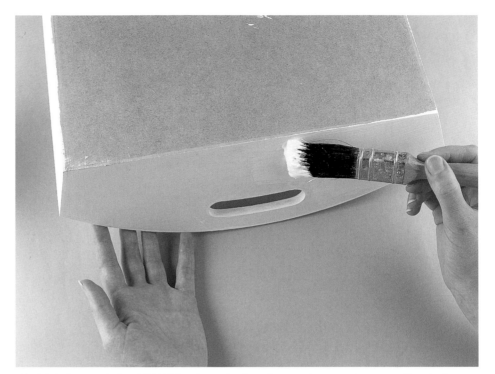

1 Lightly sand the MDF blank and wipe the surface with a muslin cloth. Prime the top of the tray and leave to dry. Once dry turn it over and prime the sides and base.

2 Line the inside edge of the base of the tray with decorators' tape.

3 Paint the base of the tray blue with two coats of emulsion, sanding between layers. Once dry, remove the decorators' tape.

4 Now use decorators' tape to protect the blue paintwork, and paint the base border and the edges of the tray with pink emulsion. Once dry, turn the tray over and paint all of the underside – also in pink.

5 Using a thin, flat-ended paintbrush, paint white edging all around the rim of the tray. Leave this to dry, then sand before painting a second coat. Allow to dry.

6 Work out the positions of your polka dots, marking lightly in pencil. Place them at roughly regular intervals. Stick the dots into position, starting with the lowest layer first.

ARTIST'S TIP

Use a pair of dividers to help work out the intervals between the polka dots.

7 Use small scissors to neatly trim the edges of the Victorian rose scraps. Play around with the roses until you have achieved a pleasing pattern.

8 Lightly mark their positions with a sharp pencil, making sure the marks will not be visible once the roses have been pasted in place. Apply paste to the back of each rose in turn and glue it into position on the base of the tray. Use a damp sponge to mop up any excess paste.

9 Smooth out the images with a spatula as you go. Once the paste has dried, use matt varnish to protect the tray. You will need plenty of coats to stand up to wet and heat, so apply at least eight layers, sanding lightly between every second coat.

FAIRY BOX

An ordinary shoebox has been transformed to make a wonderful gift for a child.

Here, Victorian flower fairy scraps decorate the lid of the emulsion-painted box. Three-

dimensional sparkle and pearl paints have been applied to add a touch of magic.

YOU WILL NEED

- Shoebox
- Decorators' tape
- Water-based primer
- Paintbrushes
- Ruler and pencil
- Pink and blue emulsion paint
- Victorian flower fairy scraps
- Reusable putty
- Cutting surface
- Scalpel
- Paste (see page 19)
- Spatula
- Sponge
- Water-based varnish
- Pink and mauve three-dimensional pearl paint
- Three-dimensional glitter paint

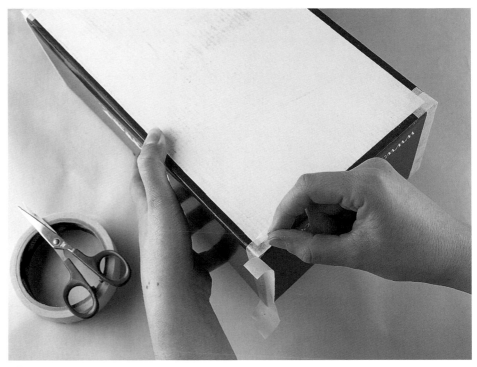

1 If the corners of the shoebox aren't neatly and securely joined, tape over them – outside and in – with decorators' tape. Don't forget to do the corners of the lid too.

2 Prime the lid and the inside of the box. Allow to dry. Then, prime the outside of the box.

3 With a ruler and pencil, mark out a border around the lid of the shoebox, and mask over with decorators' tape. Paint the centre panel of the lid with two coats of blue emulsion, and leave to dry.

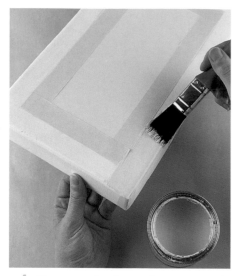

4 Remove the tape, then re-mask along the inside edges of the blue panel, so that you can paint the border and the edge of the lid with a couple of coats of pink emulsion. While the lid is drying, you can paint the outside surfaces of the box with pink emulsion.

5 Select your flower fairy scraps, and arrange them within the panel on the shoebox lid, marking out where they need to be cut and where they overlap each other. Then place on a cutting surface and cut to size using a scalpel (see page 17 for interlocking cutting).

6 Place the cutouts on the lid and mark their positions carefully with a pencil. Spread paste across the backs of the images, then press them into position and smooth over with a spatula. Wipe over with a barely damp sponge to remove any excess glue.

ARTIST'S TIP

Make sure that you spread glue right up to the edge of the images with a brush appropriate to the size of the print.

7 When the paste is dry, you can varnish the box. Apply four layers, allowing each layer to dry thoroughly before applying the next coat.

8 Once the varnish is completely dry, pipe around the edges of the panel and the box lid with little beads of three-dimensional pearl embossing paint. Alternate between pink and mauve. Do the inner edge first and leave to dry before applying the outer edge, as it is easy to smudge the paint. Finally, add the scrollwork all around the edge of the shoebox lid in three-dimensional glitter paint, and leave to dry.

DESIGN VARIATION

This box has been decorated with roses and pearls. This would be a lovely box in which to keep bridal shoes.

SKY SCREEN

Screens can be useful for all sorts of reasons – for sectioning off part of a room, for

privacy while changing, for creating ambience. Using a purpose-made MDF blank

screen, I devised a sky and seagull design using wallpaper and birds that I drew myself.

YOU WILL NEED

- MDF blank screen
- Fine sandpaper
- Face-mask
- Muslin cloth
- Water-based primer
- Paintbrushes
- Blue emulsion paint
- 2 rolls of cloud wallpaper
- Pencil
- Scissors
- Paste (see page 19)
- Spatula
- Cloth
- Cutting surface and scalpel
- Photocopies or colour printouts of seagulls (see pages 76–77)
- Reusable putty
- Matt spray varnish

1 Work with the screen in separate panels. Lightly sand the panels all over and wipe clean with a muslin cloth. Prime the edges of each screen panel and paint all visible edges with the blue emulsion. Don't bother to paint where the hinges will be fitted.

2 Unroll a section of wallpaper and lay, pattern side down, on your work surface. Place a screen panel on top and draw around it with a pencil, allowing a 1 cm (½ in) border. Cut this out.

3 Spread paste all over the wallpaper (if it is self-adhesive, follow the manufacturer's instructions.) Fold the pasted paper in half to carry it. Position the bottom corners first, allowing for the overlap, and then unfold the paper out to the top of the screen. Smooth any bubbles from the centre to the outside of the paper using a spatula. Wipe over with a damp cloth and leave to dry.

ARTIST'S TIP

Don't squeeze out too much of the paste, particularly at the edges, or the paper will lift off once dry.

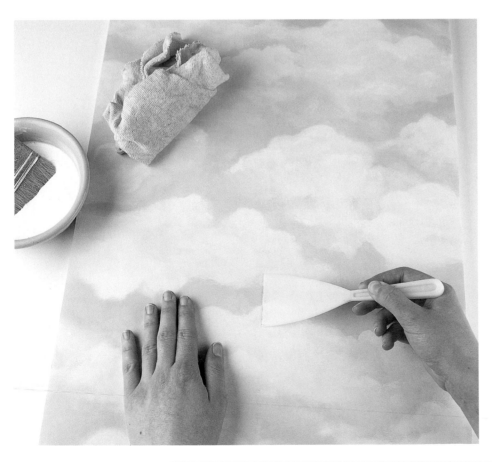

4 Lay the panel face down on a suitable surface for cutting. Using a scalpel, cut away all the excess paper, taking care not to shave the edges of the panel itself. Repeat steps 2 to 4 for both sides of all panels.

5 Photocopy or scan and print out the templates on pages 76–77. Cut them out. Use reusable putty to tack them onto the screen, playing around with them until you achieve a harmonious arrangement.

6 Carefully mark the seagulls' positions then paste them on to the screen, smoothing them down with a spatula.

ARTIST'S TIP

You may also wish to use the seagulls to decorate a bathroom wall.

7 Apply several coats of matt spray varnish. Make sure you do this in a dust-free, well-ventilated room and wear a face-mask.

8 Assemble the screen panels according to the manufacturer's instructions.

DESIGN VARIATION

Here I've used finely patterned origami paper to make and cut out clothes for this washing line. Make templates so that you can repeat the shapes. Use felt-tip pens to outline them.

FIRE SCREEN

Birds and blossoms unite to create this design, reminiscent of a more traditional découpage style. The lovely magnolias splay out across the screen while the birds perch here and there among them. Both motifs have been cut from wrapping papers.

YOU WILL NEED

- MDF blank fire screen
- Fine sandpaper
- Face-mask
- Muslin cloth
- Water-based primer
- Paintbrushes
- Cream and white emulsion paint
- Pencil and ruler
- Bird and magnolia wrapping paper
- Felt-tip pen
- Scissors
- Reusable putty
- Cutting surface and scalpel
- Pencil
- Paste (see page 19)
- Sponge
- Cloth
- Wood glue
- Water-based varnish

1 Sand the screen and wipe clean with a muslin cloth. Prime all elements of the fire screen separately and leave to dry. Paint the front and back of the screen with cream emulsion and leave to dry. Lightly sand before applying a second coat.

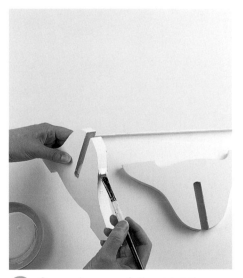

2 Once dry, carefully paint the edges of the screen and feet white. Leave to dry and repeat. Sand to ensure nice smooth edges.

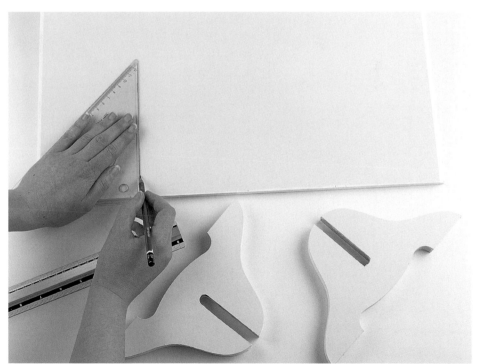

3 Use a pencil and ruler to mark positions for the feet of the screen, making sure that they are equidistant from each edge.

5 Cut out the sprays of magnolia flowers and individual birds carefully, following the instructions on pages 16–17.

4 Select the birds that you want to use from the wrapping paper, adding more detail to the images with a felt-tip pen if required.

7 Paste the backs of the images and smooth them into their marked positions on the screen. Apply the largest prints first, smallest last.

6 Arrange the prints carefully until you achieve a pleasing design. Mark out their positions with a sharp pencil, as well as any areas where they overlap. Cut the images so they will butt up against each following the instructions on page 17. This will give you a smoother, neater finish.

8 Paste all elements of the design into position one by one, wiping each with a damp sponge to catch excess glue, then drying with a cloth.

9 Glue the feet into their positions using wood glue, making sure that they sit flat on the floor. Wipe off any excess glue with a damp sponge and leave the screen to dry in a standing position. Once the feet are dry, you may want to touch up the paintwork in that area.

10 Apply four coats of varnish with a broad, flat brush. Leave each layer to dry before giving it a light sand and applying the next coat.

ARTIST'S TIP

You may wish to have a reversible screen with an alternative scene on the back to suit the season.

CHINTZ CHAIRS

These painted wooden chairs add a fresh feminine touch to any room. Choose floral fabrics to make the cushioned seats. A scan can be taken of the same fabric and used to make the découpage cutouts for the back of the chair. If you don't have access to a scanner, take the fabric to your nearest photocopy shop to have a colour copy made.

YOU WILL NEED

- Painted wooden chair
- Large sheet of scrap paper
- Pencil
- Scissors
- Old wool blanket
- Embroidery needle and thread
- Floral cushion fabric
- Sewing machine and thread
- Tape
- Needle and thread
- Photocopy of fabric design
- Paintbrushes
- Paste (see page 19)
- Spatula
- Sponge
- Water-based varnish

1 If possible remove the seat from the chair to make a pattern of it for the cushion. If you cannot do this place a large piece of paper over the seat to trace its outline in pencil and cut out.

2 Use the pattern to cut out three pieces from an old woollen blanket to make the cushion filler.

3 Sandwich the three filler layers together and blanket stitch round all the raw edges with embroidery thread. Sew crosses here and there in the centre of the "cushion filler" to stabilize the layers.

4 Fold the seat fabric in two, right sides together. Using the seat pattern, and allowing an extra 1 cm (½ in) all around, carefully cut out two pieces of fabric.

5 Tack and machine-sew a 1-cm (½-inch) hem along the back edge of each piece of fabric. Tack the two pieces together, still right sides facing, incorporating two lengths of 38 cm (15 in) tape at each of the front corners of the cushion cover. Machine-sew the sides and front of the cover, leaving the back open for inserting the blanket filler. Trim any excess tape.

6 Turn the cushion cover right-side out and press. Cut two pieces of tape 63 cm (25 in) long. Fold each in half and stitch at each corner of the back opening.

7 Place the blanket pad inside the cushion cover. Then overstitch neatly along the back opening (this can be unpicked for washing the cover at a later time).

8 Make photocopies or scans from a piece of the cushion fabric. Choose an area that will make a good motif for the back of the chair and cut it out.

9 Arrange the image on the chair, making sure that it fits neatly. Paste into position, smoothing over with a spatula, and wipe with a barely damp sponge. Leave to dry.

10 The backs of chairs get a lot of wear, so it is important that you apply a number of layers of varnish following the instructions on page 22. When the varnish is dry, you can use the tapes to secure the cushion to the chair. Adapt the size of the tape accordingly.

ARTIST'S TIP

You could also choose an image from your wallpaper to coordinate your chairs with.

JEWELLERY BOX

Chocolate foil wrappers come in wonderful, tempting colours and can be used to create

sumptuous découpage. Care must be taken when varnishing foil, as some varnishes

may remove the surface colour.

YOU WILL NEED

- MDF jewellery box blank
- Masking tape
- Fine sandpaper
- Face-mask
- Muslin cloth
- Water-based primer
- Paintbrushes
- Dark blue emulsion
- Pencil and ruler
- Confectionery foils
- Scissors
- PVA glue
- Water-based varnish

1 Cover the hinges of the box with masking tape. Sand all surfaces of the box and wipe over with a muslin cloth. Prime the box, leaving each section to dry completely before moving on to the next. Paint the inside of the box and lid with blue emulsion and leave to dry.

2 Now paint the outside edges of the lid, the base of the box and its feet blue. Paint a second coat once dry.

3 Measure all the dimensions of the box and cut a piece of foil to fit each side. Trim pieces to fit around any hinges. Glue into position.

5 Measure the top of the box lid, and cut and paste a piece of foil to fit this. Repeat for inside the lid. Leave to dry.

4 Once all the sides are glued in place, leave the box to dry completely. Cut four strips of foil to fit the corner edges of the box, and four to fit the corner edges of the lid.

6 Tear foils into shapes to make up your design for the box lid (see page 21). Here I have torn petals, leaves and stems, and other pieces for a floral pattern.

7 Cut four strips of contrasting foil to make a border for the lid. Don't worry about having them all the same thickness – a little irregularity will add to the design.

8 Arrange the basic elements of the design and glue the pieces into position.

9 Gradually build up the design, adding the flower petals, and finishing off with a circle in each corner.

10 Once all of the foil elements are completely dry, varnish the box applying at least six layers and allowing each to dry before starting the next.

ARTIST'S TIP

Easter eggs are a great source of foils. Collect them and keep them pressed smooth in a big book.

CHRISTMAS BOX

Strong self-assembly storage boxes can be purchased at some stores. If you can't find

one of these, use a stylish ready-made one. Victorian scraps and Christmas images from

a copyright-free CD have been used to decorate this box. The original rope handles were

replaced with a more suitable cord to complete the luxurious feel of the piece. Use the

box to pack away your Christmas decorations or for transporting your presents.

YOU WILL NEED

- Self-assembly box (preferably)
- Water-based primer
- Paintbrushes
- Pencil and ruler
- Decorators' tape
- Green, red, and deep purple emulsion paints
- Card
- Scissors
- Gold wrapping paper
- Paste (see page 19)
- Copyright-free images
- Victorian Christmas scraps
- Reusable putty
- Sponge
- Christmas border
- Thick gloss spray varnish
- Face-mask
- Gold cord
- Three dimensional embossing paint

1 Prime the inside of the box and lid and leave to dry before priming the outsides. Using a pencil and ruler, mark out an 8 cm (3 in) border around the top of the lid and a 5 cm (2 in) border on each side of the box, to give you a central panel on each visible surface. (The border widths can be adjusted according to the size of your box.) Mask off the borders with decorators' tape to paint the inside panel green. When dry, protect the green panel in the same way and paint the borders red.

2 Assemble the box and lid according to the manufacturer's instructions. Paint the inside of the box and lid with the purple emulsion. Leave to dry then paint a second coat. Use the template on page 77 to draw and cut out a card star. Use the template to cut stars from a sheet of gold wrapping paper. Paste them all over the interior of the box and lid at roughly regular intervals.

3 Choose the images you want to use from your copyright-free book or CD. Cut out the prints carefully and make a selection from your Victorian Christmas scraps. (An economic alternative is to use images cut out from Christmas wrapping paper.)

ARTIST'S TIP

You may prefer to use your favourite Christmas cards – this would be a great way to have them on display every Christmas.

4 Cut out the motifs for the panels on the sides of the box, making allowances for the holes that the cord handles will fit through. Taking each side in turn, tack the images to the green panel using reusable putty until you have a pleasing arrangement. Paste the images into position carefully, wiping each with a damp sponge to remove excess paste. Use little pictures where there are gaps, and remember to leave room for the Christmas border.

5 Complete the design with a Christmas border, which finishes each panel with a neat edge. This one was enlarged 50 per cent to fit the dimensions of the box. Position it and paste into place, wiping away excess paste with your sponge.

6 Choose the motifs for the lid of the box. Arrange within the green panel until you have achieved a pleasing result. Paste the images down and wipe free of any excess paste. Use the same or similar border, adjusted to the appropriate size, to complete the design.

7 Angels make a pleasant focus for the front panel of the box. Paste your chosen images according to your arrangement, and surround them with a decorative border.

8 Once all the paste is dry, varnish the box – first the inside, then the outer surfaces. Use six to eight layers of thick, gloss spray varnish, sanding lightly between every second coat to achieve a smooth finish. Be sure to wear a face-mask.

9 Thread your gold or silky cord through the holes in the side of the box, and cut the length accordingly – in this case it is 49 cm (19 in). Tie a knot in both ends of the cord to ensure it does not slip out of the holes.

10 Use three-dimensional embossing paint to edge the borders. It can be difficult doing long straight lines so make the lines slightly wiggly if you prefer.

TEMPLATES

Sky Screen (pages 56–59)

Set photocopier to 150% to copy images to correct size for project.

Christmas Box (pages 72–75)
Set photocopier to 150% to copy image to correct size for project.

SUPPLIERS

UK

Appli Craft
Hillcrest
Guilford Road
Ottershaw
Surrey KT16 0QL
General craft supplies.

The Dover Bookshop
18 Earlham Street
London WC2H 9LG
Tel: 020 7836 2111
Fax: 020 7836 1603
e-mail:
images@thedoverbookshop.com
www.doverbooks.co.uk
Royalty-free image books in fine arts
and graphic arts. Books can be
bought online.

Mamelok Press Ltd
Northern Way
Bury St. Edmunds
Suffolk IP32 6NJ
Tel: 01284 762291
Fax: 01284 703689
www.mamelok.co.uk
Scraps, diecuts, greeting cards,
friezes and garlands. Online
shopping available.

OPITEC Hobbyfix
Unit 51 Basepoint Centre
Andersons Road
Southampton
SO14 5FE
Tel: 023 80 68 24 01
www.uk.opitec.com
Complete range of craft materials,
including tweezer scissors. Online
shopping.

Scumble Goosie
Lewiston Mill
Toadsmoor Road
Stroud
Gloucestershire GL5 2TB
Tel: 01453 731305
Fax: 01453 731500
www.scumble-goosie.co.uk
Ready-to-paint and handpainted
furniture, varnishes, glazes, paints,
stencils, découpage papers and
many other craft materials. Material
can be bought on online.

The Stencil House
Phoenix Works
Vernon Road
Basford
Nottingham NG6 0BX
Tel: 0115 942 4600
Fax: 0115 942 4700
email: sales@stencilhouse.co.uk
www.stencilhouse.co.uk
Wide variety of craft and home décor
products including paints, brushes,
napkins and stencils.

William Robinson
A3 Poulton Drive
Nottingham
NG2 4BN
Tel: 0115 986 6268
email: info@williamrobinson.co.uk
www.williamrobinson.co.uk
Importers and distributors of fine wall
coverings.

Australia

ACT

Lincraft
Canberra Centre
Bunda Street
Canberra ACT 2601
Tel: (02) 6257 4516

NSW

Lincraft
Imperial Arcade
Pitt Street
Sydney NSW 2000
Tel: (02) 9221 5111

NT

Country Cottage Crafts
Shop 6-10 Smith Street
Alice Springs NT 0870
Tel: (08) 8953 3323

Spotlight Stores Pty Ltd
356 Bagot Street
Millner NT 0810
Tel: (08) 8948 2008

QLD

Lincraft
Myer Centre
Brisbane QLD 4000
Tel: (07) 3221 0064

SA

Lincraft
Level 3
Myer Centre
Rundle Mall
Adelaide SA 5000
Tel: (08) 8231 6611

TAS

Spotlight
100 Market Street
Hobart TAS 7000
Tel: 1300 305 405

VIC

Spotlight
63 Cecil Street
South Melbourne VIC 3205
Tel: (03) 9684 7477
Tel: 1300 305 405

WA

Lincraft
Carousel Shopping Centre
Cannington WA 6107
Tel: (08) 9451 5455

New Zealand

Golding Handcrafts
Rostrevor House
Marion St
Wellington
Tel: (04) 801 5855
email: golding@paradise.net.nz
www.goldingcraft.com

Hands Ashford New Zealand
5 Normans Road
Elmwood
Christchurch
Tel: (03) 3559 099
email: hands.craft@clear.net.nz
www.hands.co.nz

Spotlight Stores
Locations throughout New Zealand:
Whangarei (09) 430 7220
Wairau Park (09) 444 0220
Henderson (09) 836 0888
Pamure (09) 527 0915
Manukau (09) 263 6760
Hamilton (07) 839 1793
Rotorua (07) 343 6901
New Plymouth (06) 757 3575
Hastings (06) 878 5223
Palmerston North (06) 357 6833
Porirua (04) 237 0650
Wellington (04) 472 5600
Christchurch (03) 377 6121
Dunedin (03) 477 1478
www.spotlight.net.nz
Wide range of craft and decorative
painting supplies.

Stitch & Craft
32 East Tamaki Road
Hunters Corner
Papatoetoe
Tel: (09) 278 1351
email: sales@stitchandcraft.co.nz
www.stitchandcraft.co.nz

South Africa

Art, Stock & Barrel
Shop 44, Parklane Centre
12 Commercial Road
Pietermaritzburg 3201
Tel: 033 342-1026

The Crafters Den
17 2nd Avenue
Orange Grove 2192
Johannesburg
Tel: 011 483-0563

Crafty Arts
Walmer Park Shopping Centre
Port Elizabeth 6001
Tel: 041 368-2528

Crafty Supplies
Shop UG 2, Stadium on Main
Claremont 7700
Cape Town
Tel: 021 671-0286

Découpage Studio
49 Umhlanga Rocks Drive
Durban North 4051
Tel: 031 564-9288

Jimnettes Art and Craft
42 Lynridge Mall
Lynnwood Road
Lynnwood Ridge 0081
Pretoria
Tel: 012 361-4469

Talents
Shop 2, Medene Centre
60 2nd Avenue
Westdene 9301
Bloemfontein
Tel: 051 430-1127

Acknowledgements
The author would like to thank:

Frederick Warne & Co. – controls all rights in the Flower Fairies books on behalf of the estate of Cicely Mary Barker.

The Medici Society for permission to use their fairies wrapping paper by Margaret Tarrant.

Pete Andrew and **Kathryn Hughes** at **WAVE**, Buckfastleigh and **James Gillmore**, **John** and **Eric** for their help with the computer.

Cath Lucroft Mee for use of the fabric bunting shown on pages 2 and 64.

Andrew Gillmore and **Heidi Green** for looking after Bryany during the photography.

The author would also like to thank the following companies for supplying materials for use in this book: **Appli Craft, Dover Publications Inc. (31 East 2nd St, Mineola, NY 11501, http://store. doverpublications.com/), Mamelok Press Ltd, OPITEC Hobbyfix, Scumble Goosie, The Stencil House** and **William Robinson.**

INDEX